Mensa® KiDS

TRAIN your BRAIN

PUZZLE BOOK

LEVEL 1
FOR BEGINNER PUZZLERS

THIS IS A CARLTON BOOK

Text and puzzle content copyright © British Mensa
Limited 1994 & 1997 & 2010
Design and artwork copyright © Carlton Books Limited
1994 & 1997 & 2010 & 2014

This edition published in 2014 by Carlton Books Limited
An imprint of the Carlton Publishing Group
20 Mortimer Street, London, W1T 3JW

10 9 8 7 6 5 4 3 2 1

A catalogue record for this book is available from the British Library.

ISBN 978-1-78312-073-4

Printed in Dongguan, China

Senior Editor: Alexandra Koken
Designed by: Katie Baxendale
Production: Marion Storz

Mensa KIDS

TRAIN your BRAIN PUZZLE BOOK

LEVEL 1

FOR BEGINNER PUZZLERS

CARLTON KiDS

INTRODUCTION

SO YOU WANT TO TRAIN YOUR BRAIN?

This little book will get your grey cells in shape in no time.

This **LEVEL 1** puzzle book is packed with questions to test your verbal and numerical reasoning. To solve them you'll need the ability to think logically, plus some staying power when the problems get tough.

Now, put on your thinking cap, turn the page and let the training begin!

LEVEL 1 is the first in the Train Your Brain Puzzle Book series: check out **LEVEL 2** for intermediate and **LEVEL 3** for advanced puzzles.

WHAT IS MENSA?

Mensa is the international society for people with a high IQ. We have more than 100,000 members in over 40 countries worldwide. The society's aims are:

* to identify and foster human intelligence for the benefit of humanity
* to encourage research in the nature, characteristics, and uses of intelligence
* to provide a stimulating intellectual and social environment for its members

Anyone with an IQ score in the top two per cent of the population is eligible to become a member of Mensa – are you the "one in 50" we've been looking for? Mensa membership offers an excellent range of benefits:

* Networking and social activities nationally and around the world
* Special Interest Groups – hundreds of chances to pursue your hobbies and interests – from art to zoology!
* Monthly members' magazine and regional newsletters
* Local meetings – from games challenges to food and drink
* National and international weekend gatherings and conferences
* Intellectually stimulating lectures and seminars
* Access to the worldwide SIGHT network for travellers and hosts

For more information about Mensa:
www.mensa.org.uk
Telephone: +44 (0) 1902 772771
E-mail: enquiries@mensa.org.uk
British Mensa Ltd., St John's House, St John's Square,
Wolverhampton, WV2 4AH

PUZZLE 1

Move up or across from the bottom
left-hand 1 to the top right-hand 1.
Collect nine numbers and add them together.
What is the highest you can score?

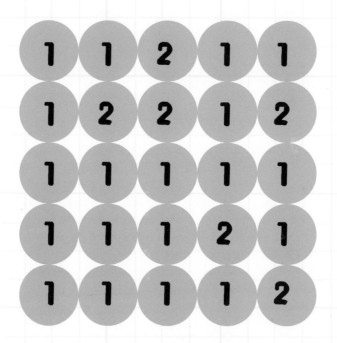

PUZZLE 2

Replace the question mark in the circle above with the missing letter.

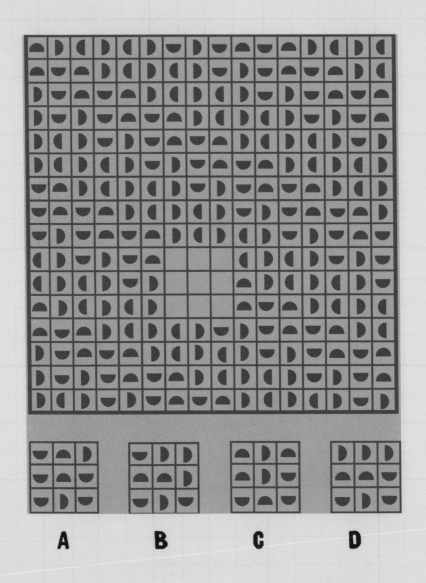

A   B   C   D

PUZZLE 3

Which of these patterns fits into
the blank section?

8

PUZZLE 4

Join together the dots using odd numbers only. Start at the lowest and discover the object. What is it?

6

17 1

3

5

15

11

8

13

2

7

9

PUZZLE 5

Can you find the number which comes next in this sequence?

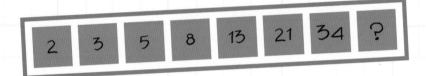

2   3   5   8   13   21   34   ?

PUZZLE 6

Correct this equation by moving one match.

IV − VI = II

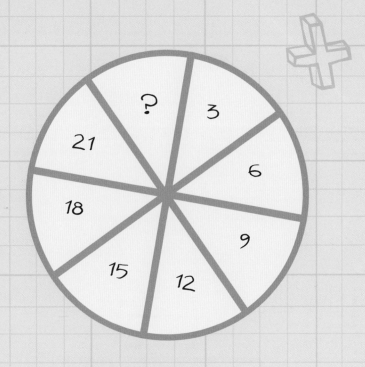

PUZZLE 7

Replace the question mark with the missing number in the circle above.

WHOOP! WHOOP!

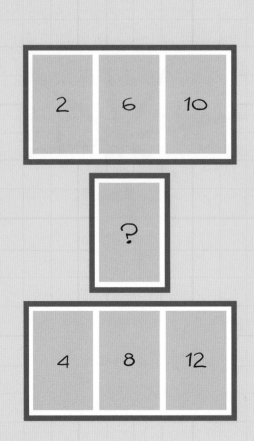

PUZZLE 8

Place in the middle box a number larger than 1. If the number is the correct one, all the other numbers can be divided by it without leaving any remainder. What is the number?

PUZZLE 9

Which of the following cubes
cannot be made from this layout?

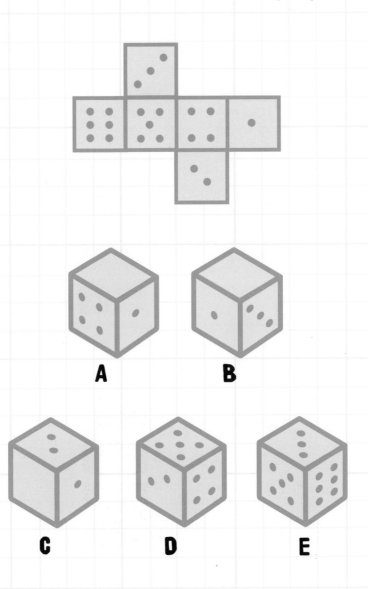

A

B

C

D

E

PUZZLE 10

Replace the question mark with
the missing number.

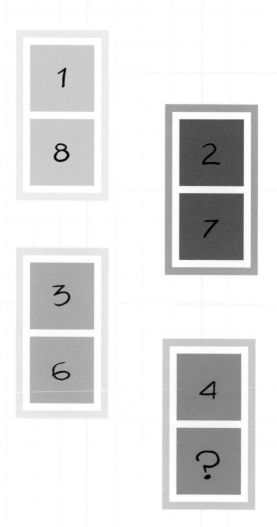

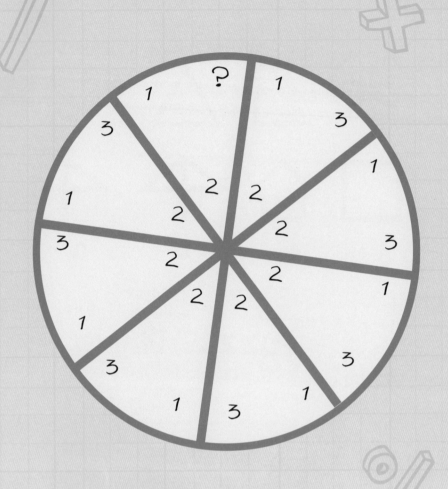

PUZZLE 11

Each sector of the circle follows a pattern.
What number should replace
the question mark?

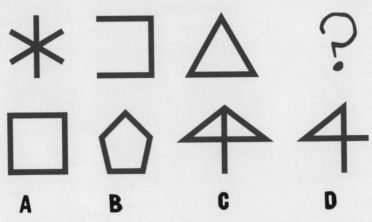

A   B   C   D

PUZZLE 12

Which figure should replace the question mark?

I'M GETTING INTO THE SWING OF THIS!

PUZZLE 13

Replace the question mark with a number to meet the conditions of the wheel.

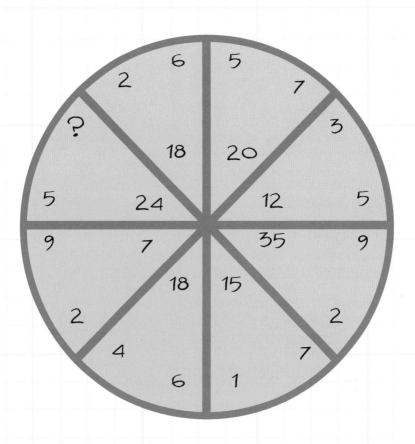

PUZZLE 14

Here is an unusual safe. Each of the buttons must be pressed only once in the correct order to open it. The last button is marked F. The number of moves and the direction are marked on each button. Thus 1U would mean one move up, whilst 1L would mean one move to the left. Which button is the first you must press? Here's a clue: it can be found on the top row.

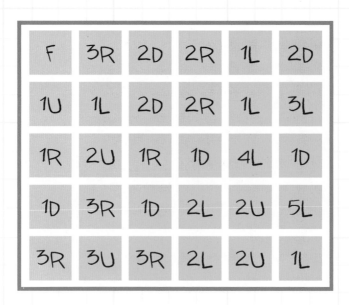

F	3R	2D	2R	1L	2D
1U	1L	2D	2R	1L	3L
1R	2U	1R	1D	4L	1D
1D	3R	1D	2L	2U	5L
3R	3U	3R	2L	2U	1L

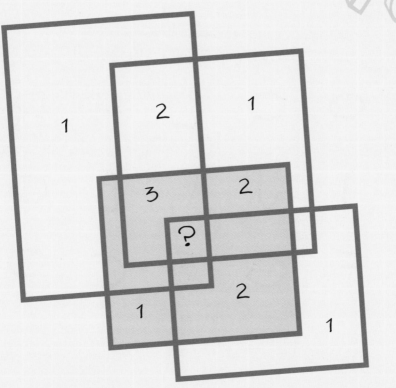

1   2   1

3   2

?

2

1   2

1

PUZZLE 15

This diagram was constructed according to a certain logic. Can you work out what number should replace the question mark?

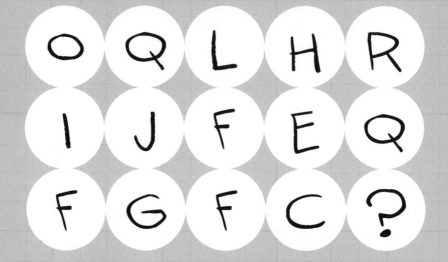

O Q L H R
I J F E Q
F G F C ?

PUZZLE 16

Can you find the letter which completes the diagram?

PUZZLE 17

Each slice of this cake adds up to the same number. What number should replace the question mark?

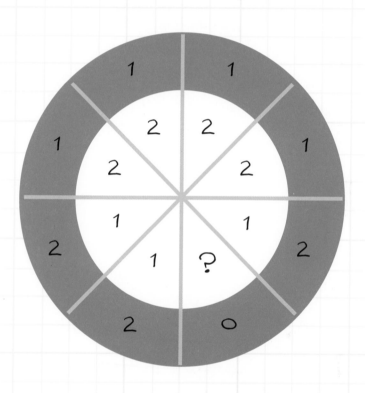

OOH, TRICKY ONE!

PUZZLE 18

Work out the relationship of the letters and numbers in this square and find out what number should replace the question mark.

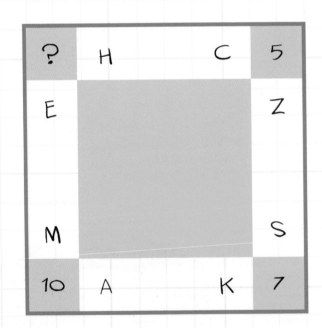

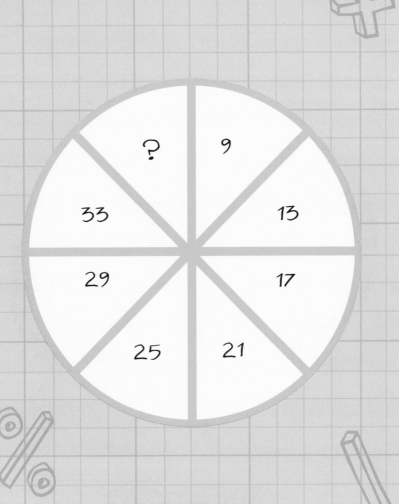

PUZZLE 19

Find the missing number to replace the question mark in the circle above.

PUZZLE 20

Copy out these shapes carefully and rearrange them to form a number.
What is it?

Can you find the number to go at
the bottom of triangle D?

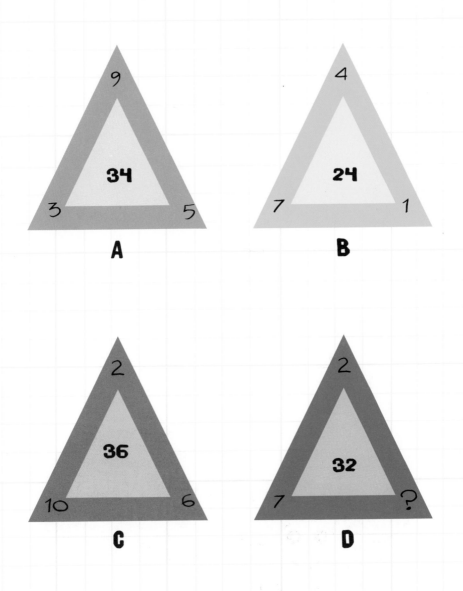

PUZZLE 22

Look at the pattern of numbers in the diagram. What number should replace the question mark?

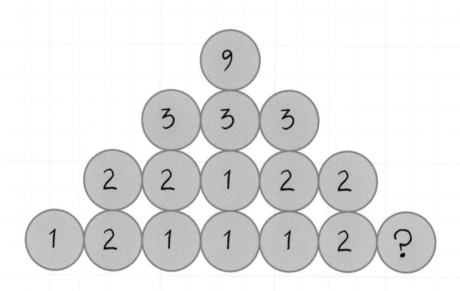

YOU'VE ALMOST GOT IT!

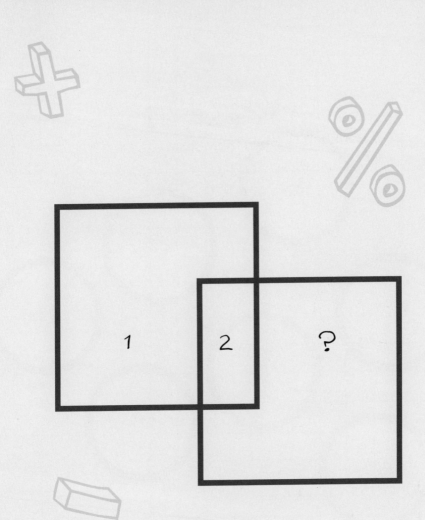

1   2   ?

PUZZLE 23

If you look carefully you should see why the numbers are written as they are. What number should replace the question mark?

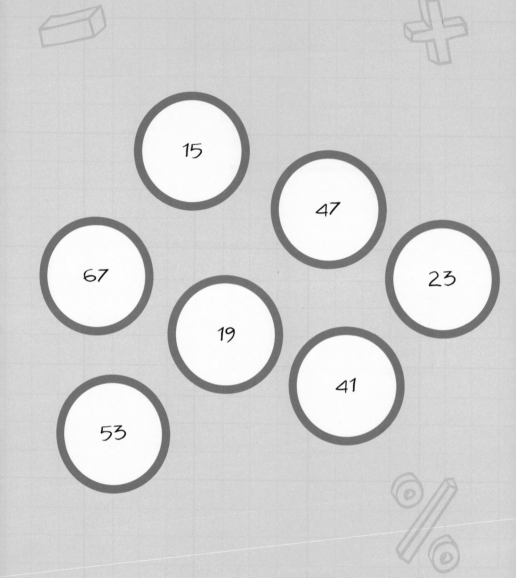

PUZZLE 24

Which is the odd ball out?

PUZZLE 25

Can you work out the time on the blank clock face?

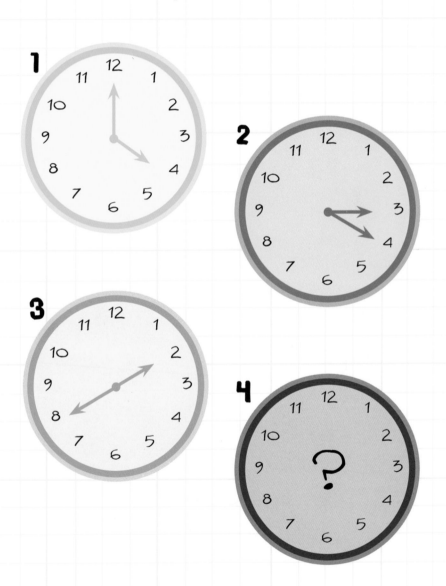

PUZZLE 26

Work out how the numbers in the triangles
are related and find the missing number.

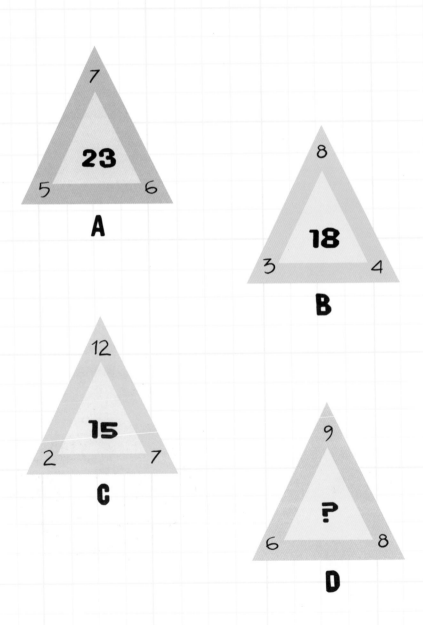

PUZZLE 27

In this diagram, starting from the top of the diamond and working in a clockwise direction, the four basic mathematical signs (+, −, x, ÷) have been omitted. Restore them so that the calculation, with answer in the middle, is correct.

I'M FEELING BRAINY TODAY!

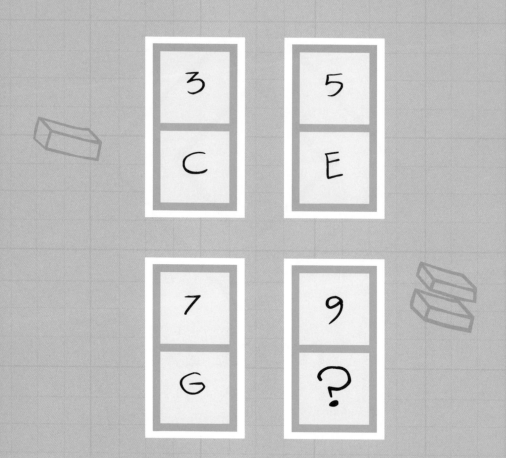

PUZZLE 28

Replace the question mark in the box above with the missing letter.

PUZZLE 29

Move from the bottom left-hand 3 to the top right-hand 3 adding together all five numbers. Each pink circle is worth 1 and this should be added to your total each time you meet one. What is the highest total you can find?

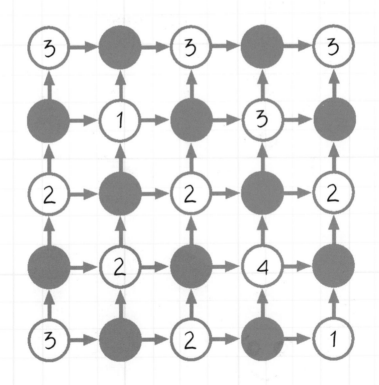

PUZZLE 30

The numbers in each sector of the wheel are linked in some way. Find the number needed to replace the question mark.

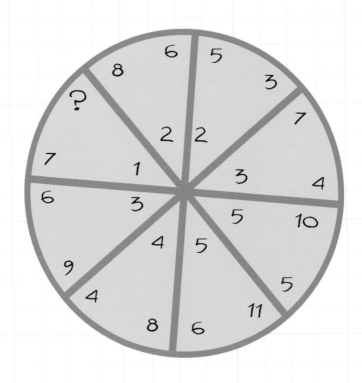

THINK HARD!

PUZZLE 31

The numbers and letters in this square are linked. Find the correct number to replace the question mark. It will help if you think of the alphabet laid out in a circle, rather than a straight line.

1	1	1	3
1	2	1	4
2	2	3	7
3	1	2	?

A   B   C   D

PUZZLE 32

The numbers in column D are linked in some way to those in A, B and C. What number should replace the question mark?

PUZZLE 33
What is the time on the fourth watch?

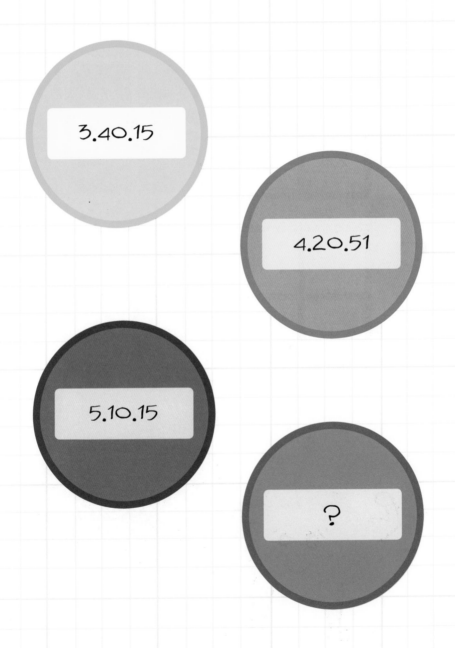

3.40.15

4.20.51

5.10.15

?

PUZZLE 34

Find the missing number in the puzzle below.

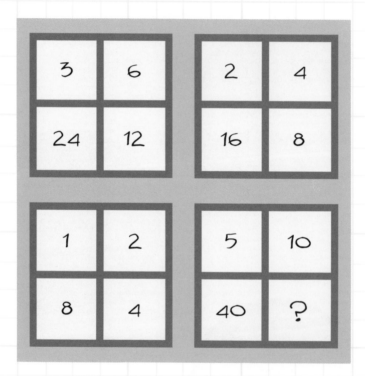

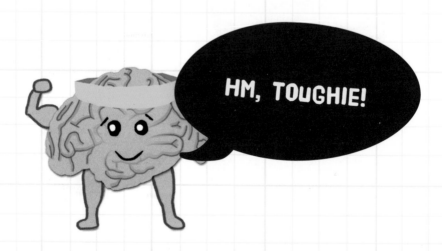

HM, TOUGHIE!

PUZZLE 35

Start at the A and move to B passing through various parts of the rhinoceros. There is a number in each part and these must be added together. What is the lowest total you can find?

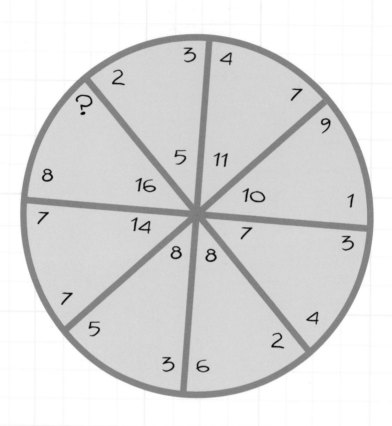

PUZZLE 36

Replace the question mark with
the missing number.

PUZZLE 37

Which figure is the odd one out?

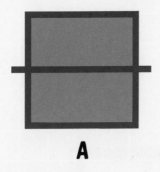

A

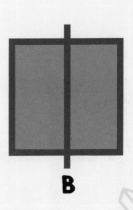

B

C

D

PUZZLE 38

Each symbol is worth a number. The total of the symbols can be found alongside each row. What number should replace the question mark?

8

20

4

?

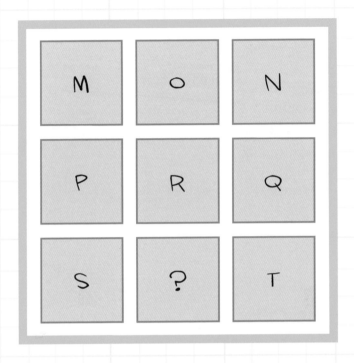

PUZZLE 39

Find the missing letter. Is it K, U or J?

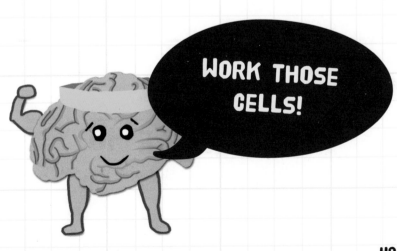

WORK THOSE CELLS!

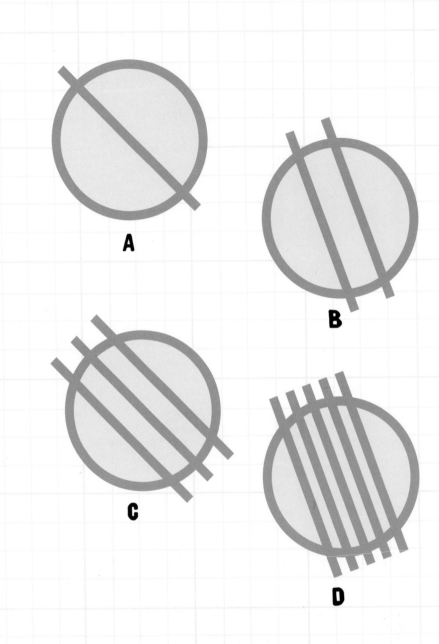

A

B

C

D

PUZZLE 40
Which circle is the odd one out?

PUZZLE 41

On the planet Venox the coins used are 1V, 2V, 5V, 10V, 20V and 50V. A Venoxian has 85V in his squiggly bank. He has the same number of three kinds of coin. How many of each are there and what are they?

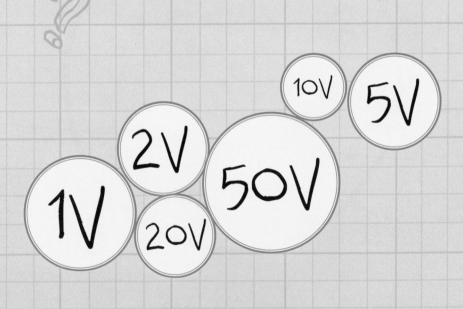

PUZZLE 42

Which is the odd number out in the circle below?

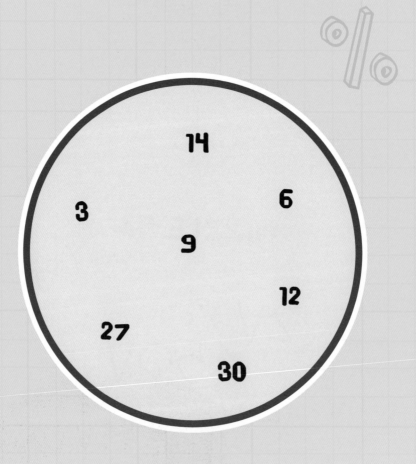

14

6

3

9

12

27

30

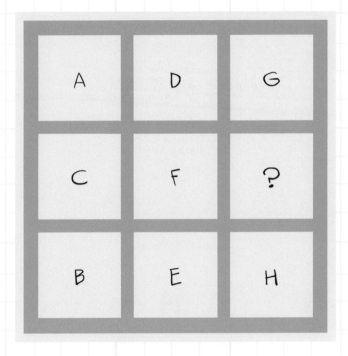

PUZZLE 43
Find the missing letter. Is it I, K or N?

HALFWAY THROUGH!

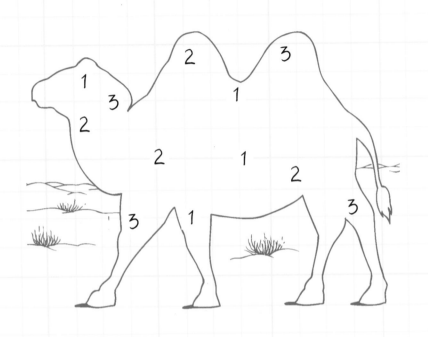

PUZZLE 44

What is the lowest number of straight lines needed to divide the camel so that you can find the numbers 1, 2 and 3 in each section?

PUZZLE 45

Find the symbol that will balance the
last set of scales.

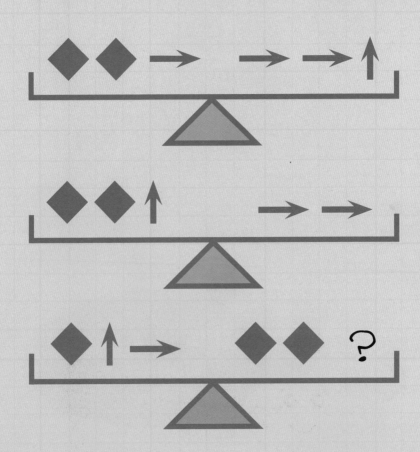

PUZZLE 46

Which is the odd face out?

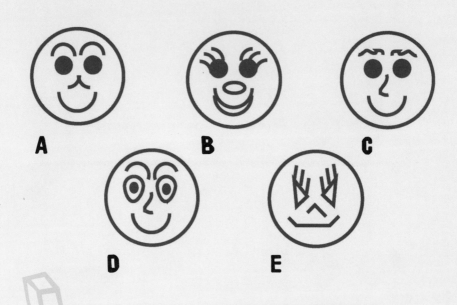

A

B

C

D

E

THIS IS A GREAT WORKOUT!

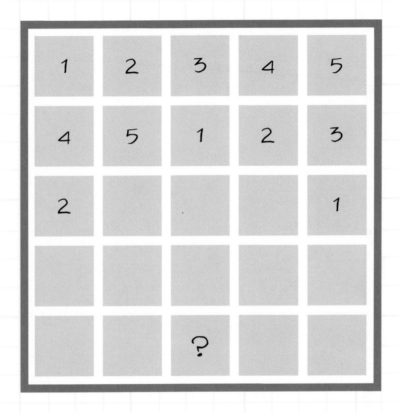

PUZZLE 47

Fill up this square with the numbers 1 to 5 so that no row, column or diagonal line of five squares uses the same number more than once. What number should replace the question mark?

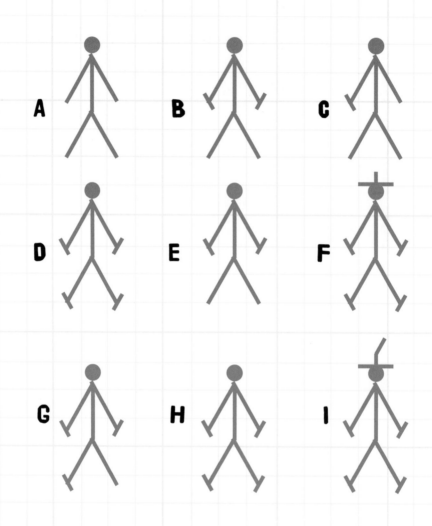

A

B

C

D

E

F

G

H

I

PUZZLE 48
Which matchstick man, G, H or I, would carry on the sequence?

PUZZLE 49

A curious logic governs the numbers in these circles. Can you discover what it is and then work out what the missing number should be?

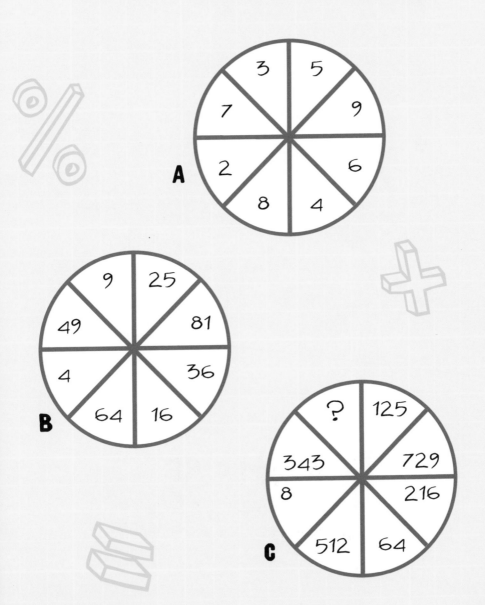

PUZZLE 50

Follow the arrows and find the longest possible route. How many boxes have been entered?

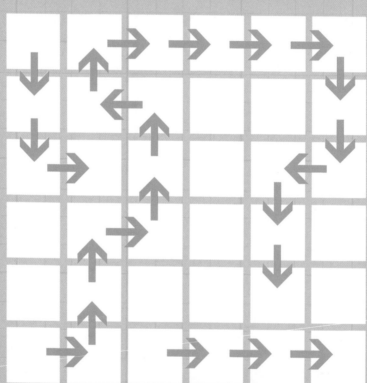

PUZZLE 51

These clocks move in a certain pattern.
What is the time on the last clock?

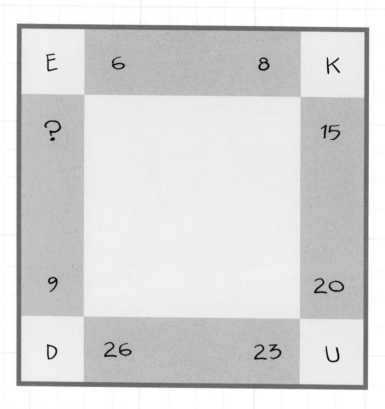

PUZZLE 52

The letters and numbers in this square follow a pattern. What number is represented by the question mark?

PUZZLE 53

The symbol on the flag will give
a number. What is it?

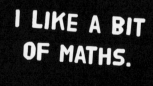

I LIKE A BIT
OF MATHS.

PUZZLE 54

Which of the symbols in this puzzle
would balance the third scale?

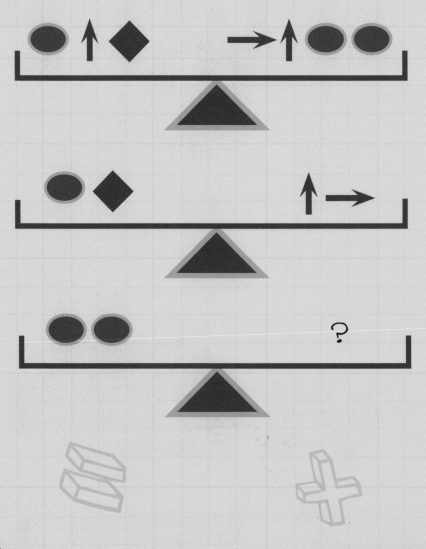

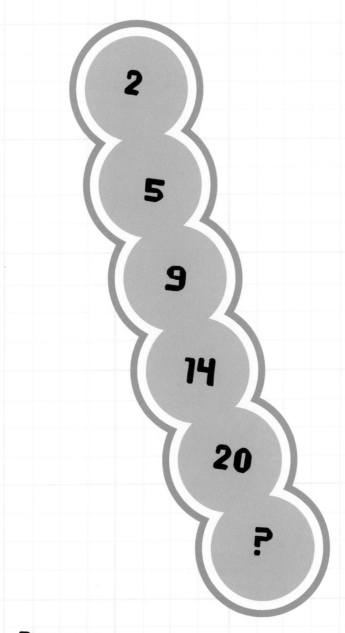

PUZZLE 55
Complete this series
of numbers.

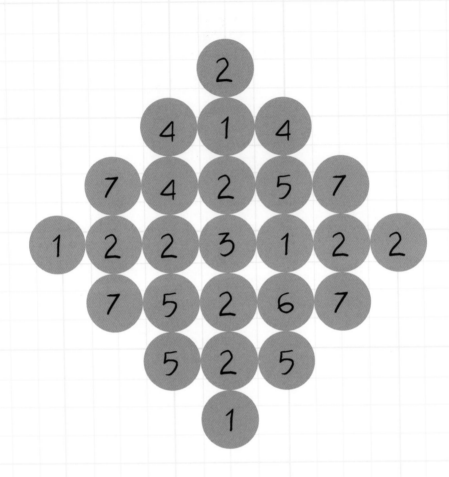

PUZZLE 56

Start at the middle 3 and move from circle to touching circle. Collect three numbers and add them to the 3. How many different routes are there to make a total of 8?

PUZZLE 57

A section of this grid has been removed and its symbols deleted. Replace the symbols so that the logic of the grid is restored.

+	+	−	−	−	÷	÷	×	×	×	+	+	−	−	−	÷
×	+	+	−	−	−	÷	÷	×	×	×	+	+	−	−	÷
×	+	−	−	−	÷	÷	×	×	×	+	+	−	−	−	×
×	+	÷	÷	×	×	×	+	+	−	−	−	÷	−	÷	×
÷	×	−	+	−	−	−	÷	÷	×	×	×	÷	÷	÷	×
÷	×	−	+	×	+	+	−	−	−	÷	+	×	÷	×	+
−	×	−	×	×	×	+	+	−	−	÷	+	×	×	×	+
−	÷	+	×	×	×	+	−	−	−	×	−	×	×	×	−
−	÷	+	×	÷				−	÷	×	−	+	×	+	−
+	−	×	÷	÷				×	÷	×	−	+	+	+	−
+	−	×	÷	−				−	+	+	÷	−	+	−	÷
×	−	×	−	−	−	+	+	×	×	×	÷	−	−	−	÷
×	+	÷	−	−	−	+	+	×	×	×	÷	÷	−	−	×
×	+	÷	−	−	−	+	+	×	×	×	÷	÷	−	÷	×
÷	×	×	×	÷	÷	−	−	−	+	+	×	×	×	÷	×
÷	−	−	−	+	+	×	×	×	÷	÷	−	−	−	+	+

PUZZLE 58

Which two sides on these cubes
have identical numbers?

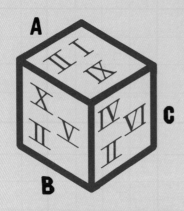

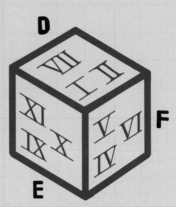

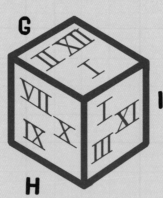

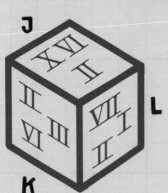

PUZZLE 59

How many squares of any size can you find in this diagram?

PUZZLE 60

Turn the number shown on the calculator into 32 by pressing two buttons only. What are they?

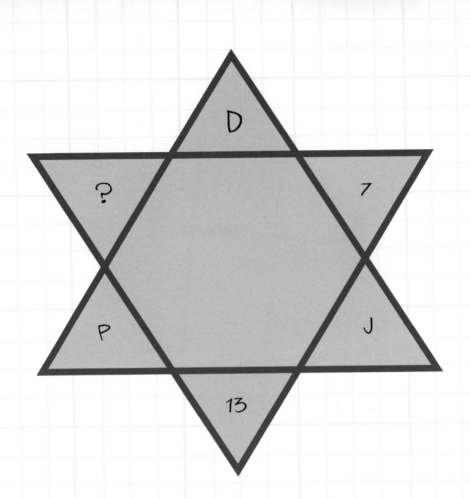

PUZZLE 61

Find the number to complete the diagram.

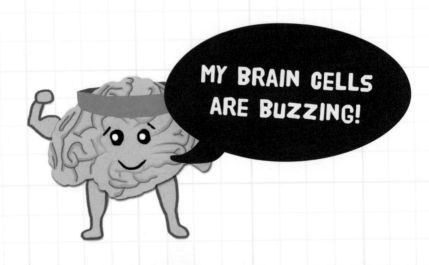

MY BRAIN CELLS ARE BUZZING!

PUZZLE 62

Can you work out whether + or − should replace the question marks in this diagram so that both sections arrive at the same value?

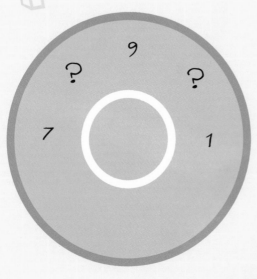

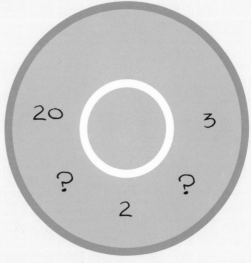

PUZZLE 63

The first set of scales balance. How many
As will make the second set balance?

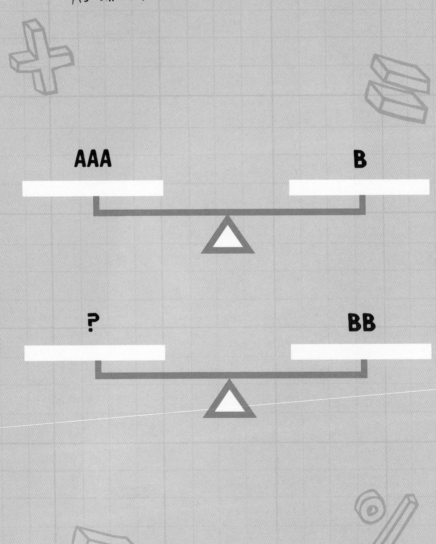

AAA   B

?   BB

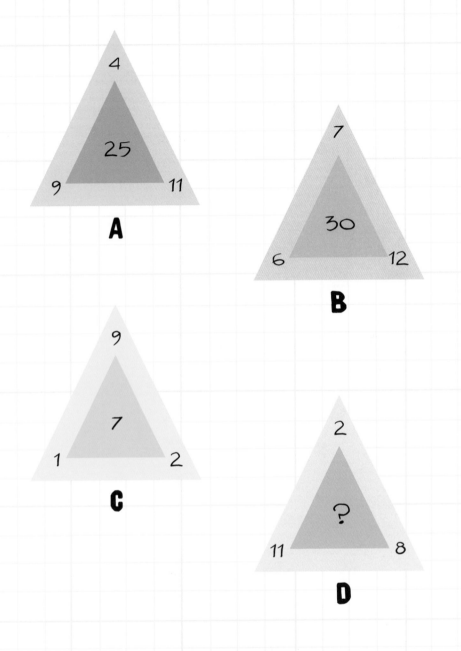

PUZZLE 64

The above triangles follow a pattern. Can you work it out and find the missing number?

A IS TO   **B AS**   **C IS TO**

D   E   F   G

PUZZLE 65

Is the answer D, E, F or G?

YOU'RE GETTING GOOD AT THIS!

PUZZLE 66

Divide up the box using three lines so that each shape adds up to the same total. How is this done?

2	5	5	9
8	9	2	5
5	8	9	2
9	2	8	8

PUZZLE 67

Each symbol in this square represents a value. Can you work out the total represented by the question mark?

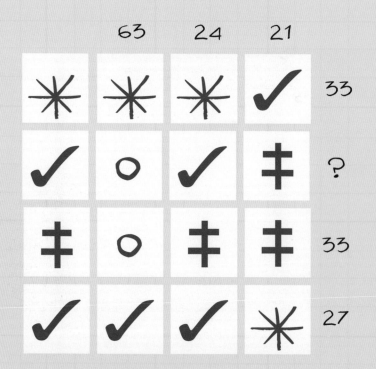

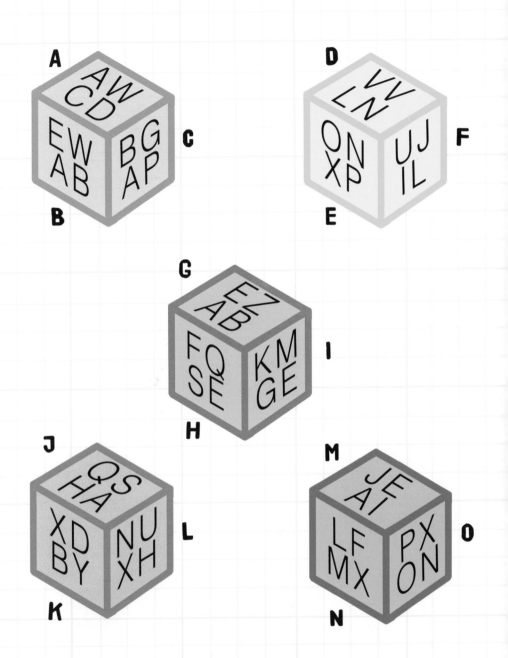

PUZZLE 68

Two sides of these cubes contain the same letters. Can you spot them?

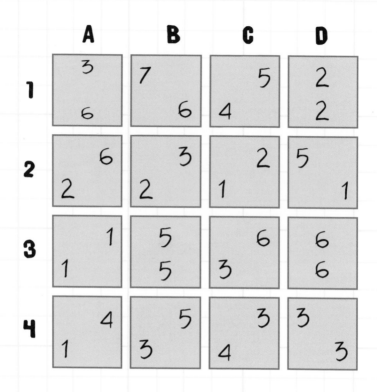

	A	B	C	D
1	3 6	7 6	5 4	2 2
2	6 2	3 2	2 1	5 1
3	1 1	5 5	6 3	6 6
4	4 1	5 3	3 4	3 3

PUZZLE 69

Which squares contain the same numbers?

I KNOW THIS ONE!

PUZZLE 70

Which letter fits in the missing segment?

73

PUZZLE 71

There is a logic to the patterns in these squares but one does not fit. Can you find the odd one out?

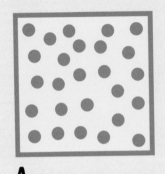

A

B

C

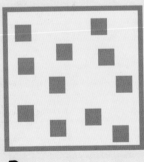

D

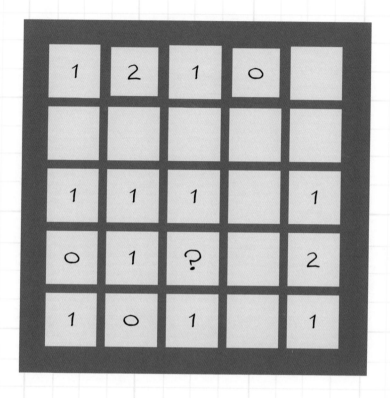

PUZZLE 72

Fill in the empty boxes so that every line adds up to 5, including the lines that go from corner to corner. What number should replace the question mark?

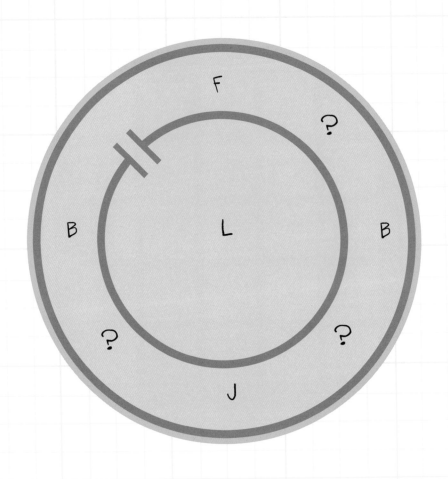

PUZZLE 73

Can you work out which mathematical signs should replace the question marks in this diagram? You have a choice between − or +.

PUZZLE 74

Which letter replaces the question mark in this star?

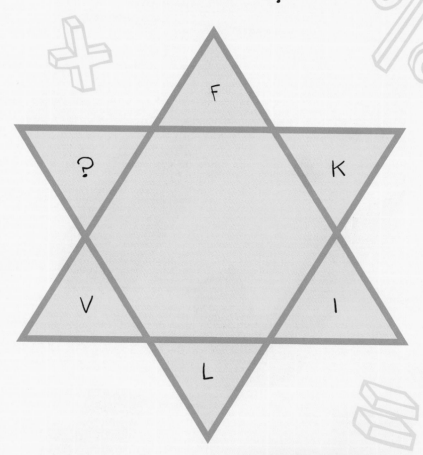

TEST A FRIEND ON THIS ONE!

PUZZLE 75

Copy out these shapes carefully and
rearrange them to form a number.
What is it?

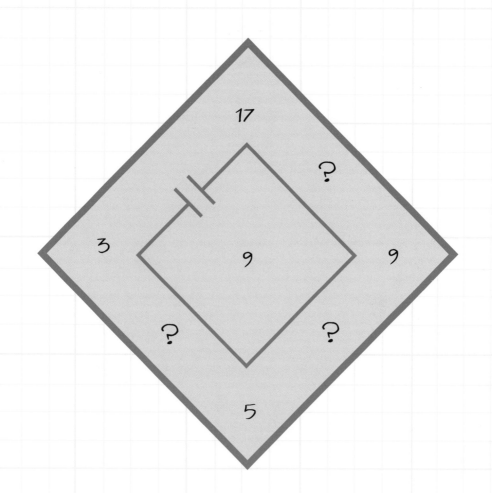

PUZZLE 76

The mathematical signs in this diamond have been left out. Reading clockwise from the top, work out what the question marks stand for.

PUZZLE 77

Which of the faces A, B or C would carry on the sequence above?

WHOOP! WHOOP!

PUZZLE 78

What number should be placed in the triangle to continue the series?

2

4

6

?

PUZZLE 79

Here is a series of numbers. What number should replace the question mark?

| 1 | 2 | 3 | 1 | 2 | ? | 1 |

PUZZLE 80

Can you work out what number should go into the last square?

7   14

35

28   21

4   8

20

16   12

6   12

30

24   18

3   6

?

12   9

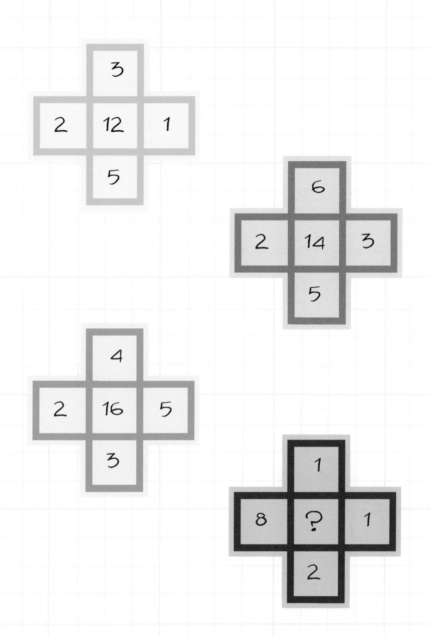

PUZZLE 81

Find a number to replace the question mark.

PUZZLE 82

Replace each question mark with plus, minus, multiply or divide. Each sign can be used more than once. When the correct ones have been used the sum will be completed. What are the signs?

| 1 | ? | 1 | ? | 3 | | = | 5 |

PUZZLE 83

How many 3s are inside this Pterodactyl?

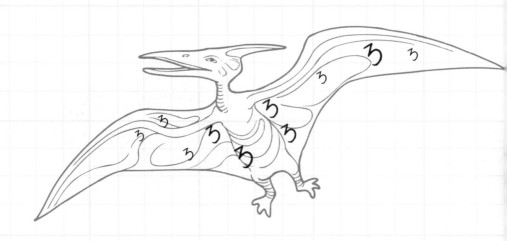

PUZZLE 84

Which of these diagrams is the odd one out?

YOU'RE GETTING GOOD AT THIS!

PUZZLE 85
What comes next in this sequence?

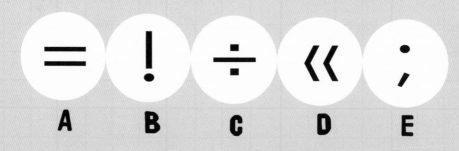

| A | B | C | D | E |

PUZZLE 86
Can you work out which of these symbols is the odd one out?

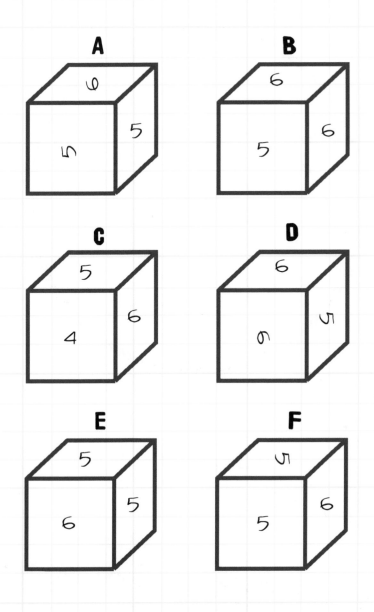

PUZZLE 87

Which of these pictures is not of the same box?

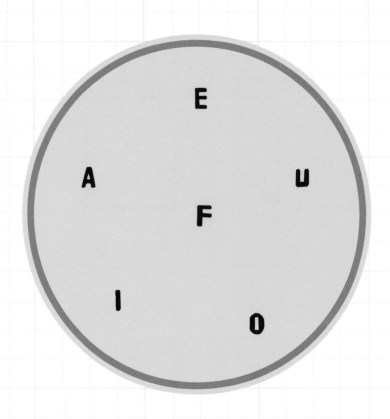

PUZZLE 88

Which letter in the circle is the odd one out?

WORK THOSE CELLS!

PUZZLE 89

Find the correct six numbers to put in the frame. There are two choices for each square, for example 1A would give the number 2. When the correct numbers have been found an easy series will appear. What is the series?

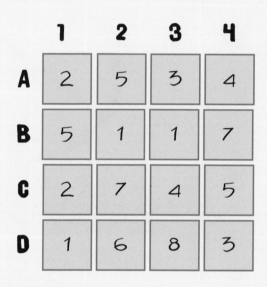

	1	**2**	**3**	**4**
A	2	5	3	4
B	5	1	1	7
C	2	7	4	5
D	1	6	8	3

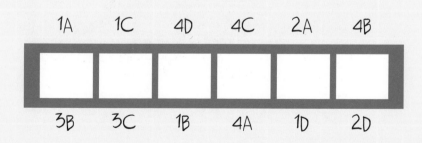

1A	1C	4D	4C	2A	4B
3B	3C	1B	4A	1D	2D

PUZZLE 90
Which of these figures is the odd one out?

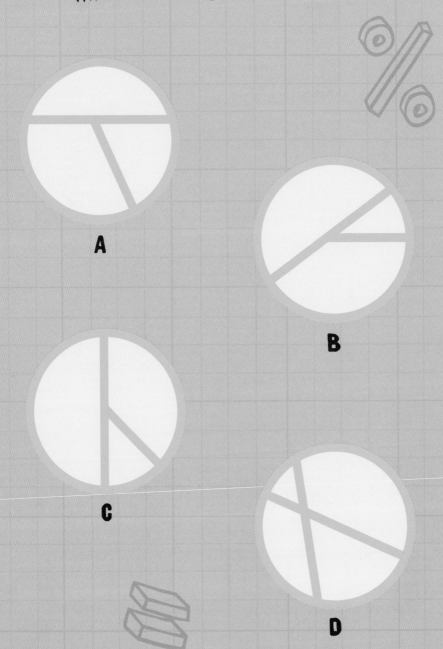

A

B

C

D

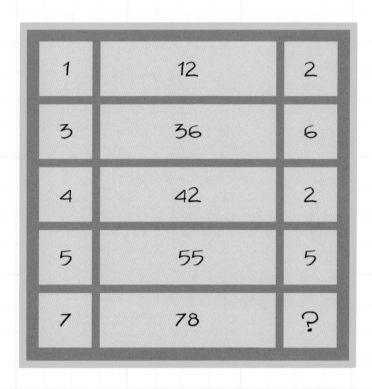

1	12	2
3	36	6
4	42	2
5	55	5
7	78	?

PUZZLE 91

The numbers in the middle section have some connection with those down the sides. Find out what it is and work out what should replace the question mark.

ANSWERS

ANSWER 1
12.

ANSWER 2
0. Reading clockwise from the top, miss one letter each time.

ANSWER 3
A. Pattern is: 2 with the arch on top, 4 with the arch at right, 3 with the arch on bottom, 2 with the arch at left. Start at the top left corner and move down the grid in vertical lines, reverting to the top when of the next column when you reach the bottom.

ANSWER 4
A hammer.

ANSWER 5
55. Add the two last numbers together.

ANSWER 6

ANSWER 7
24. Reading clockwise from the top, each number increases by 3.

ANSWER 8
2.

ANSWER 9
E.

ANSWER 10
5. The numbers in each domino add up to 9.

ANSWER 11
3. Each sector contains the numbers 1, 2 & 3.

ANSWER 12
D. All the figures can be made with 3 lines.

ANSWER 13
4. Multiply the two numbers in the outer circle of each spoke and place the product in the inner circle two spokes on in a clockwise direction.

ANSWER 14
2D, in the third column.

ANSWER 15
4. The number relates to the number of shapes in which the number is enclosed.

ANSWER 16
A. Letters represent values based on their position in the alphabet. In each column, subtract the letter in the middle row from the letter in the top row and place the answer in the bottom row.

ANSWER 17
3.

ANSWER 18
8. Starting at H, and working clockwise, subtract the value of the second letter, based on its value in the alphabet, from the value of the first letter, and put the sum in the following corner.

ANSWER 19
37. Reading clockwise from the top, add four each time.

ANSWER 20
3.

ANSWER 21
7. Add the three numbers at the corner of each triangle, multiply by 2 and place that number in the middle.

ANSWER 22
1. The pattern is symmetrical.

ANSWER 23
1. The number is surrounded by only one shape.

ANSWER 24
15. None of the other numbers have a divisor — they are all prime numbers.

ANSWER 25
1.00. The minute hand moves forward 20 minutes, the hour hand moves back 1 hour.

ANSWER 26
21. Add all the numbers of each triangle together and place the sum in the middle of next triangle. When you reach D put the sum in A.

ANSWER 27
$6 + 7 + 11 \div 3 \times 2 + 5 - 12 = 9$.

ANSWER 28
I. Go to 9. Each letter corresponds in alphabetic position with the number above it. I is the 9th letter.

ANSWER 29
19.

ANSWER 30
6. Reading clockwise in each segment subtract the second number from the first and put the answer in the middle.

ANSWER 31
6. The numbers represent the number of letters between the corner letters, in alphabetical order.

ANSWER 32
6. Add together A, B and C to get D.

ANSWER 33
6.05.51. The hours increase by one, minutes are divided by two and the seconds reverse digits each time.

ANSWER 34
20. Starting from the top left corner, the numbers double at each step in a clockwise direction.

ANSWER 35
11.

ANSWER 36
8. The numbers on the rim of each sector are added together and the answer is put in the middle.

ANSWER 37
D. All the other squares are divided exactly in half.

ANSWER 38
8.

ANSWER 39
U. In each row the letters form a continuous alphabetic series in the order: left, right and middle.

ANSWER 40
B. All the other circles are crossed by an odd number of lines.

ANSWER 41
5 of 2V, 5V and 10V coins.

ANSWER 42
14. All the others are divisible by 3.

ANSWER 43
I. Reading across each row, miss two letters at a time.

ANSWER 44
2.

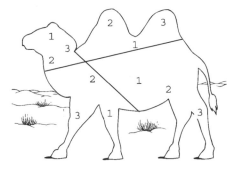

ANSWER 45
A diamond.

ANSWER 46
E. It contains no curved lines.

ANSWER 47
5.

ANSWER 48
G. Add 2 elements to the body, take away 1, add 3, take away 2, add 4, take away 3.

ANSWER 49
27. A number in the first circle is squared and the product is put in the corresponding segment of the second circle. The original number is then cubed and that product is put in the corresponding segment of the third circle.

ANSWER 50
18.

ANSWER 51
6.45. The minute hand moves back 15, 30 and 45 minutes. The hour hand moves forward 3, 6 and 9 hours.

ANSWER 52
10. Replace each letter by the value of its position in the alphabet. Start at E and add 1, then 2, then 3, then 4, then 5, then 1, then 2 etc. When you reach 26 (Z), go back to 1 (A).

ANSWER 53
3. A 3 and its mirror image are placed together.

ANSWER 54
One arrow pointing up.

ANSWER 55
27. $2 + 3 = 5 + 4 = 9 + 5 = 14 + 6 = 20 + 7 = 27$.

ANSWER 56
4.

ANSWER 57

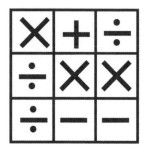

The order is 2 +, 3 −, 2 ÷, 3 x. The puzzle goes in an inward clockwise spiral starting from the top left corner.